Farm Machines

Harvesters

Connor Dayton

PowerKiDS press.

New York

Published in 2012 by The Rosen Publishing Group, Inc.
29 East 21st Street, New York, NY 10010

First Edition

Editor: Jennifer Way
Book Design: Greg Tucker

Photo Credits: Cover, pp. 5, 6–7, 11, 15, 16–17, 19, 21, 23, 24 (top left, top right, bottom right) Shutterstock.com; pp. 8–9, 24 (bottom left) © McPHOTO/age fotostock; pp. 12–13 © www.iStockphoto.com/Dmitry Kalinovsky.

Library of Congress Cataloging-in-Publication Data

Dayton, Connor.
 Harvesters / by Connor Dayton. — 1st ed.
    p. cm. — (Farm machines)
 Includes index.
 ISBN 978-1-4488-4948-2 (library binding) — ISBN 978-1-4488-5046-4 (pbk.) —
ISBN 978-1-4488-5047-1 (6-pack)
 1. Harvesting machinery—Juvenile literature. I. Title.
 TJ1485.D39 2012
 633.1'045—dc22

2010048479

Manufactured in the United States of America

CPSIA Compliance Information: Batch #WS11PK: For Further Information contact Rosen Publishing, New York, New York at 1-800-237-9932

Contents

Harvesters pick grain **crops**. Picking crops is called harvesting.

Harvesters pick crops like corn and wheat. Most American wheat is grown in Kansas.

The **header** is at the
front of the harvester.

The header feeds the crops into the harvester.

The crops are cut.
Then they fall into
the harvester.

The harvester frees the grain. Everything else falls back onto the **field**.

The grain stays in the harvester. Soon it fills up.

The harvester has a pipe. The grain flows through the pipe.

The grain goes into **trailers**. Then the grain is stored.

Harvesting is hard work.
Harvesters make it easier!

Words to Know

crops

field

header

trailer

Index

Web Sites

Due to the changing nature of Internet links, PowerKids Press has developed an online list of Web sites related to the subject of this book. This site is updated regularly. Please use this link to access the list:
www.powerkidslinks.com/farm/harvest/